Journey to Peace

Journey
—— *to* ——
Peace

[31 Devotions Through the Grief of
Miscarriage, Stillbirth, or Other
Pregnancy Loss]

Keanna Barnes

Gold Peach Press

Los Angeles • Atlanta

Gold Peach Press
P. O. Box 341011
Los Angeles, CA 90034
www.YourPeaceJourney.com

First printing 2016
Printed in the United States of America

ISBN-13: 978-0-9979057-0-0
ISBN-10: 0-9979057-0-0

Library of Congress Control Number: 2016914351

For my first born son,
Nathanael Elias Barnes
"EJ"

CONTENTS

INTRODUCTION

Let me first take a moment to wrap my arms fully around you while we take a deep breath and exhale slowly. Please excuse my tears. There are no words, no gifts, nothing that could bring back what you have lost. Since going through my own pregnancy loss, I've heard and read so many touching, heartbreaking stories from men and women sharing their own similar, yet very unique and personal tragic experiences. At the time, I didn't realize how often these traumatic events take place. I didn't realize how many people walk around silently carrying the weight of the pain and the unspeakable emotion that comes with pregnancy loss. It was this complex, complicated grief that left me searching for hope, searching for comfort, searching for peace, searching for…God.

Once I gained enough strength to speak freely about what I had been through without sobbing uncontrollably (like the really, really ugly loud cries that would make anyone around really uncomfortable), I was able to understand that I could reach out to those who were also suffering. I could pray for you for comfort, encourage you to keep your head up and help you look to God for the strength and healing to get you to your "new normal" in Christ. A tragic event in life can shake our world to the core and because of it, you can bet that you will be forever changed.

The purpose of this book is to help you get to a point

of peace with your loss and with God. Broken into five sections, you take a proactive role in your path to PEACE:

- **Pray**: Take your anxiety, fears, and anger to God in prayer
- **Entrust**: Know that God can handle your emotions, feelings, and questions
- **Act**: Use practical ways to release your emotions
- **Change:** Transform your mind and gain a new outlook on life
- **Encourage**: Be an encouragement to others who are suffering

Life is a journey, and pregnancy loss can put a crack in your path and in your heart. If you want to turn your hurt into hope, your fear to faith, your loss to love and your pain to peace, this book is for you.

This book is designed so that you can meditate daily on each scripture within the sections for a month, or at your own pace, and come back to each meditation as needed along your journey. I've also created a journal to accompany this book. Your complimentary journal will be an important guide to help you through the passages and exercises in the book. The journal can be downloaded at: www.YourPeaceJourney.com.

The thoughts I share in the following pages are raw and are a direct reflection of how I felt very soon after my pregnancy loss while in the midst of my healing. Take as much time as you need with the passages and remember to breathe as you revisit your own experience. It's okay to cry. It's okay to pray. It is my hope and prayer that you will use this book as one of the many tools you will need as you push through your pain to find peace and allow God to heal your heart.

MY STORY

When I was pregnant, I had many fears. One of my fears was labor and delivery. This fear was so intense that I would have very graphic dreams about it. To try to ease my outlook, I would ask other mothers about their child's birth. Everyone had a different variation of the same story. Some were quick, easy, and heavily medicated, while others were long, painful, and begging for mercy. No matter how the birth went, they all agreed that once they heard the cries of their precious baby, that it was all worth it. All nine months of sickness, swollen ankles, stretch marks, watchful eating, doctor visits, and labor pains melted once they held their babies close.

What happens when the mother's expectations are destroyed? What about the women who go through the expectation, the pain, and the labor only to be met with silence and the most sobering quiet in the delivery room. The only cries are from the mother. The mother who knows that when this baby is delivered she won't hear a thing. How does she forget the pain? How can she say that the labor and anticipation was all worth it?

It was a Tuesday. I had just returned to bed from one of my frequent 4:00 am restroom breaks and even though I laid there for an hour, I could not go back to sleep. It bothered me to just lie there with my mind racing since there was so much I needed to do. I had to go to work in a couple of hours so I got up and decided to make calls to my insurance companies about doctor bills they needed to cover. This was probably not a great way to start the day as the calls left me very frustrated. I got ready for work, and since I was up so early, I had time to stop for a breakfast sandwich on my way. I waddled into work still grumpy from unproductive insurance calls but content with my full stomach. As I rolled my chair as close to my desk that my 27 week belly would allow, I was sure that my son was also happy that I had a good breakfast when I felt him kicking. I had a prenatal appointment scheduled for early that afternoon so I hurried to condense my work day in half. This was my last appointment before I entered my third trimester so I was looking forward to going to the doctor. The stress of my compacted schedule was heightened by phone calls from angry people taking their frustrations out on me. In addition, there were numerous interruptions that prevented me from getting what I needed to get done, leaving me overly stressed and frustrated. Normally, I'm not an overly emotional person, but the pregnancy hormones got me going and I struggled to hold back tears as I worked through my anxiety. I left in time to grab a bite to eat before my appointment. The traffic was moving slowly but my heart was racing as I rushed to the doctor's office to meet my husband who was there waiting for my arrival. The nurse called me in to check my weight and blood pressure. We made small chat as she wrapped my arm and pressed buttons on the machine. She stopped abruptly and stared at the monitor with wide eyes. "Well, your blood pressure is way too high!" she exclaimed. I explained that I had a stressful morning and I asked her to take it again as I breathed deeply and prayed silently trying to calm myself down. She took it again and she shook her head telling me that the second reading was higher than the first. She took me to an empty room and asked me to lie on my left side and wait for my doctor to see me. I did as I was told with my husband by my side as he tried to help me de-stress. I tried to block my worried thoughts and only focus on breathing as we waited. When my doctor came in, the nurse showed her my blood pressure readings and she looked more wide-eyed than the nurse did. They both agreed that I needed to go to the adjoining hospital. I was still unaware of what this all meant, but I could feel my anxiety growing because of the concern they were showing. My doctor wanted to check our baby's heartbeat before I headed across the street. She brought out the monitor and glided it across my belly as we all waited to hear. And we waited. And waited. My breath quickened as I stared at my doctor's perplexed face. "I don't...I don't..." Her voice was almost a whisper and she asked the nurse to bring another doctor into the room. By now, my brain was in full panic mode. My husband, being very optimistic, mumbled that our baby was probably hiding from us. I knew in my heart, that wasn't the case, but I held on hoping that he was right. The second doctor came in, and with the monitor, carefully rolled it across me searching for a sign of life. She slowly turned to my doctor, shook her head and quickly walked out. I could feel heat coming from my body and sweat beading on my forehead. I stared blankly at my doctor as I waited for her confirmation. She looked at me solemnly, "I'm sorry Keanna, but there is no heartbeat." I felt my body grow limp as I wailed loud enough for heaven to hear me. My husband and doctor grabbed hold of me as they tried to console me. They might as well have told me that they didn't hear my heart beating either because that was the moment when my world stopped.

Unknowingly, I developed preeclampsia, which is marked by high blood pressure, protein in urine, swelling, headache, and other symptoms that are normal in pregnancy. Preeclampsia is a very dangerous complication that can claim the lives of both mother and baby. Even though it can also appear postpartum in a woman, delivery is the only cure for preeclampsia. This dreaded delivery that once haunted my dreams had immediately become a real life nightmare.

The next few days were a blur. My mother flew in from across the country as doctors induced labor while giving me high doses of magnesium to combat my soaring blood pressure. I vomited from the medical concoctions they pumped through my veins. I was a limp, sorrowing rag in their hands and I was numb with pain. Not the pain from my condition or from the methods they used to keep me alive, but it was the pain from the death that had taken place inside. It was the pain of my broken heart. My son was gone and so was a part of me.

I prayed, cried, and questioned God, demanding answers and understanding. It was not until I began searching the scriptures that I slowly gained hope, faith, and comfort in God's love. I invite you to look to God's word as we go through this life-long journey of pushing past our pain to God's promise of peace.

[P]ray

E

A

C

E

DAY ONE

> ⁶ Do not be anxious about anything, but in every situation, by prayer and petition, with thanksgiving, present your requests to God. ⁷ And the peace of God, which transcends all understanding, will guard your hearts and your minds in Christ Jesus.

Philippians 4:6-7

Our human need and desire to understand "why" this happened to us and to our baby seems to aim itself at providing closure to our tragedy. The problem comes when our question is unanswered—the doctors had no viable explanation to offer us other than "sometimes it just happens." I wanted answers. I needed to know answers. I knew that nothing "just happens." I also knew that no answer would have been good enough for me. I knew that my baby was gone and no answer would bring my baby back. This passage spoke to the anxiety and depression caused by my loss. Philippians 4 offers both a command and a promise. The command is to take your requests and frustrations and emotions to God. Once you go to God in prayer, you should expect that the peace of God, the peace that exceeds all limits of thought, will watch over and protect your broken heart and troubled mind. God wants you to give Him everything you got. All of your thoughts, questions, fears, anxieties, sadness, guilt, weakness…whatever you have, give it to Him. He is able to reign down a peace in your heart and mind that is far greater than any answer we desire.

> I needed to know answers.

DAY TWO

[¹² Be joyful in hope, patient in
affliction, faithful in prayer.]

Romans 12:12

Is it even possible to be joyful and patient when you feel as if your heart has been ripped out and torn in two? So on top of everything that has unfolded and transpired, I'm expected to be joyful and patient???

This is a difficult concept to grasp in the midst of grief. The last thing you want to hear about is being joyful and patient. God understands. He is asking us to be joyful in hope and our hope is in Christ—not in our unfortunate circumstances. Our joy is in the hope and the expectation and the knowledge that this battle, this suffering, is all in the hands of God. We can rest assured that God hears our prayers, that He sees our tears, that He feels our pain. In it all He asks us to be patient, to be steadfast. I believe that the only way we can achieve this peace in such dire situations is that we look to Him. He asks us to be faithful in prayer. We have to pray for the guidance in how to act and what this joy and patience looks like in our new normal that we are forced to face every day without our precious little child. We have to pray for the strength to endure and for the comfort and peace that only He can provide.

> God understands.

DAY THREE

[7 Cast all your anxiety on him because
he cares for you.]

I Peter 5:7

If we are not careful, grief can completely consume us and take over, becoming bigger than God in our life. Grief is very natural and very necessary in our healing—even Jesus wept! We grieve because we care and because we love. We must not forget that God cares for us and loves us even more than we love

> We grieve because we care and because we love.

and care for ourselves and for the child we loss. The devil will want us to remain stuck in depression, brokenness, and hopelessness forever. We can't fool ourselves into thinking that we can handle all of the emotion that comes with pregnancy and infant loss all by ourselves. We must trust that not only does God care for us, but that He has the power to restore us. To "cast" something means to let it go. If I'm holding my jacket and I cast it to the sofa, that means I'm not holding on to it anymore. The sofa is now responsible for the weight of my jacket. God wants the responsibility of holding our heart, sorrow, sadness, and heartache.

DAY FOUR

[
¹⁸ And pray in the Spirit on all
occasions with all kinds of prayers and
requests. With this in mind, be alert
and always keep on praying for all the
Lord's people.
]

Ephesians 6:18

Sometimes, I think that we think that God can't handle what we feel, or how we feel. We forget that God knows our thoughts

> We forget that God knows our thoughts before we think them.

before we think them. He knows our feelings and emotions because He gave them to us! He knows that we are angry, confused, and deeply hurt by our loss. In the days following my loss, I was so very angry. I was steaming mad. I felt robbed – robbed of the hopes and dreams I had for my baby, robbed of the future visions I created for my family, robbed of the celebrations and joy that come with parenthood. I felt robbed of one of the greatest responsibilities of this world. My knowing that even crackheads gave birth to beautiful babies made me even madder. I told all this to God (even about the crackheads). He listens. He listens because He cares and He loves us. We weren't designed to keep all of our complicated thoughts and emotions bottled up inside. We are not God. We have a God who is waiting for our individual responses to our grief with open arms. He can restore our emptiness with hope, peace, and love.

DAY FIVE

[
¹⁶ Rejoice always, ¹⁷ pray continually,
¹⁸ give thanks in all circumstances;
for this is God's will for you in Christ
Jesus.
]

I Thessalonians 5:16-18

In the mornings, before we start the hustle and bustle of our day, my husband usually says a prayer. His prayers vary depending on what is going on in our lives and in the lives of our family and friends. In his prayers following our loss, I would hear him thanking God for our experience. Hearing this would literally wake me up out of my sleep. My heart would pound and I could hardly wait for him to finish before I questioned him about this peculiar prayer: "Why in the world would you thank God for this?" I quizzed him as I tried, unsuccessfully, to hold back tears. He very calmly explained that he was grateful for the joys that we did receive during the pregnancy. The joy of finding out that we were pregnant, the joy of learning that we were having a boy, every appointment we went to with ultrasounds and heartbeats and all ten fingers and toes as we watched our son dance around on the monitor. My husband was very thankful. I rolled my eyes because even though I knew that he was right, I found it very hard to be thankful. This scripture asks us to be thankful in __all__ circumstances.

> My husband was very thankful.

"Even this one God?" It says in all circumstances, not just the circumstances that give us the warm and fuzzies. Job says in Job 2:10, "Shall we accept good from God, and not trouble?" My husband reminded me how blessed we are and that we need to praise God no matter our outlook or situation.

DAY SIX

⁹ Be merciful to me, Lord, for I am in
distress;
my eyes grow weak with sorrow,
my soul and body with grief.
¹⁰ My life is consumed by anguish
and my years by groaning;
my strength fails because of my
affliction,
and my bones grow weak.

Psalm 31: 9-10

As my worst fear was confirmed by my doctor (and with two other doctors because of my disbelief), I cried in the most agonizing way possible, I continued to cry daily, sometimes uncontrollably. This unexpected, complicated grief can completely engulf and overwhelm your spirit. It is in times such as these that we cry out to God. God can handle your tears, your questions, your interrogations of Him and His ways, your immense pain, your anger, your confusion, your frustration, your distress.

> O what peace we often forfeit,
> O what needless pain we bear,
> All because we do not carry
> Ev'rything to God in prayer

-Joseph Scriven

DAY SEVEN

> 12 For our struggle is not against flesh
> and blood, but against the rulers,
> against the authorities, against the
> powers of this dark world and against
> the spiritual forces of evil in the
> heavenly realms.

Ephesians 6:12

Sometimes anger can be misdirected. When it was confirmed that my first born baby no longer had a heartbeat, I was angry. I was mad at God. It took me a while, but slowly I came to remember that God is love. God is life. Anything and anyone that is in opposition with life and with love is not of God. We are in a constant war against powers that are fighting for our souls. "The thief comes only to steal and kill and destroy" (John 10:10) and as followers of the Creator, we are prime target for his schemes. The devil loves to attack when we are weak. He attacks our homes, relationships, our minds, and our hearts. We have to stay alert to what is going on in our lives and stay strong in Christ. Staying prayerful to God in our weakest moments continually strengthens us with the power we have of the Holy Spirit through Christ. You are not fighting this battle alone. You have access to the mighty power of the most high to help you through this painful and difficult period in your life. The same power that performed miracles and conquered death is in you as you are in Him.

> We are in a constant war against powers that are fighting for our souls.

PEACE PRACTICE #1

When you first found out you were pregnant, you may have been excited and happy, or surprised and scared, or all of the above. Your mind may have wondered if you were going to have a boy or girl, or how your child would look and act. Perhaps you talked to your baby about what was going on in your world and how much you looked forward to your due date.

Write a letter to your baby. A real old fashioned letter. It doesn't have to be long. You can let your child know the love that you will always have for him or her and how you cherished the brief time you had together. Tell your child everything you wanted to say but never got the chance to say. This is your chance.

PRAYER

Lord, I pray that you wrap your loving arms around me and engulf me with your love, mercy, and healing power. I ask that you bless me with a peace so great, that it transcends understanding. Strengthen me, as I am weak with sorrow. Guide me through my struggles and pain. Help me to remain faithful as I hold on to your word and your promises. Though I mourn my loss, I pray for joy in the hope and expectation of great things in my life, knowing that my suffering is not in vain. I cast all of my anxiety to you so that I do not have to carry that burden any longer. God, I have so much to be thankful for and I thank you in advance for what is to come.

Amen.

P
[E]ntrust
A
C
E

DAY EIGHT

[
33 "I have told you these things, so that
in me you may have peace. In this
world you will have trouble. But take
heart! I have overcome the world."
]

John 16:33

God never said that His children would live a life free of trouble, pain, and grief. As a matter of fact, he promises just the opposite. He tells us that we *will* have trouble. The difference is that though we have experienced this great pain and agony, we can have peace. If we lived lives in which, everything went our way, and there was no sadness, no grief, no trouble, no sin, no distress, no problems, then there would be no need for God in our life. The reality is that because this life guarantees suffering and turmoil we *need* God in our lives so that we can have peace. This peace does not come from within but it comes from without. We are without cribs, without lullabies, without fond memories of tiny hands and feet, without loud cries and soft giggles. Even though we are without, we can have peace within Christ.

> This peace does not come from within but it comes from without.

Because we are just human and subject to frailties, we need God to equip us for His glory. The peace that we need to overcome our trouble can only be found in Him. God has already overcome the world. Surely He will be victorious in restoring our broken hearts.

DAY NINE

²² Because of the Lord's great love we
are not consumed,
for his compassions never fail.
²³ They are new every morning;
great is your faithfulness.
²⁴ I say to myself, "The Lord is my
portion;
therefore I will wait for him."

³¹ For no one is cast off
by the Lord forever.
³² Though he brings grief, he will show
compassion,
so great is his unfailing love.
³³ For he does not willingly bring
affliction
or grief to anyone.

Lamentations 3:22-24; 31-33

When you are in the midst of grief, it can be hard to see and feel God's love. We know that God's love is greater than we could ever imagine, and that He is faithful in being compassionate to us

> God's love is greater than we could ever imagine

in our time of sorrow. Compassion is not only a feeling of sympathy when someone is suffering, but it is also acting on the sympathy in order to help whoever is suffering. This passage promises that God will show compassion towards you in your grief. You can trust that His compassion is continuous and that we can expect it daily. Receiving compassion from God with His infinite power, love, grace, and mercy is sufficient for your grief.

DAY TEN

> ¹⁹ And my God will meet all your needs according to the riches of his glory in Christ Jesus.

Philippians 4:19

With a pain so great, we may feel the need to be whole again, we may feel the need for love, for understanding, and for peace. Philippians 4 tells us that God will meet all of our needs. Not some, but all. As followers of Christ, we have access to God and to God's authority and power. It is as if we walk around with an "all access" pass around our necks. Whatever we are in need of we can trust that God will provide. Comfort to our hearts? Compassion in our suffering? Joy in the midst of our pain? Patience to wait on Him expectantly? He will provide.

He will provide.

DAY ELEVEN

[
7 The Lord is my strength and my
shield;
my heart trusts in him, and he helps
me.
My heart leaps for joy,
and with my song I praise him.
]

Psalm 28:7

It is easy to have confidence in doctors and in our own knowledge. What if we had that same full confidence and trust in God? It is easy to get caught up in what we are told to avoid and

> What if we had that same full confidence and trust in God?

what precautions should be taken when we are pregnant. We should, of course, take special care and follow what is good for us, but we should also look to God. When the doctors fail us and when they have no answers for our tears, we should keep looking to God. God strengthens us, He protects us, and He provides our every need. We can have full confidence and trust that God will help us through our difficult, unexplainable times. In Him we have joy and we give thanks because He sustains us.

DAY TWELVE

[
^{13} May the God of hope fill you with all
joy and peace as you trust in him, so
that you may overflow with hope by
the power of the Holy Spirit.
]

Romans 15:13

God's word is full of promises. Have you ever broken a promise? Of course you have! God is a keeper of His word. When we trust and have faith that God hears our prayers, that He sees our tears, and that He is compassionate towards our grief, we are promised that our God will fill us with joy and with peace. In filling us with joy and peace, we will have an abundance of hope. As long as we have hope we don't give up! When we have hope, we can get rid of any guilt and shame because God can replace it with joy, peace,

> We have hope that His promises will never fail.

and hope. We have hope that His promises will never fail. His power and His love are forever and they are available to you.

DAY THIRTEEN

[
¹ You have searched me, Lord,
and you know me.
² You know when I sit and when I rise;
you perceive my thoughts from afar.
]

Psalm 139:1-2

I love my husband dearly, but I'm not taking notes on each time he sits down and gets back up (I'm just very glad that he can do these things). Every feeling, every emotion is known by God. Mundane actions that we take for granted like sitting and standing are important to God. The trauma that we feel is also important to God. The thoughts you think are known by God before they even cross your mind. My loss was a huge blow to my self-confidence. One of the thoughts I had in my loss was that I must have been unworthy to be a mother. I placed my worth on my womb and my ability to bring forth life. I felt that this was punishment for something I had done. I felt ashamed, guilty, and unworthy. If pregnancy loss is punishment, then I don't think people would even exist, considering that everyone is guilty of something. God values you so much that He cares about every aspect of your life. Your value does not come from your ability to produce children but it comes from who you are in Christ. Your value is not based on your abilities or anything physical. God loves you because you are His. He

> God values you so much that He cares about every aspect of your life.

knows you inside and out. And He *still* loves you. You are valuable, and precious in His sight. He even gave up His son for you. Knowing firsthand how hard it is to lose a child, I can appreciate how great His love is.

DAY FOURTEEN

[
¹¹ For I know the plans I have for you,"
declares the Lord, "plans to prosper
you and not to harm you, plans to give
you hope and a future.
]

Jeremiah 29:11

God has a purpose and a plan for your life. We also have plans for our own life. If you were to think back on your life and how you once thought your life should be versus the reality of how your life has unfolded, I'm sure they don't quite line up the same. I'm also sure that if we all had our way with our life, we would be in serious trouble. Fortunately, we have a God whose eyes can see what we cannot. We have a God who is not only compassionate, but who has great plans for us and for our future—the future that He sees. Your loss may have been unexpected, but it was not a surprise to God. He knew that you would need great comfort and peace in this difficult time. He knew that you would need reassurance that no soul goes unnoticed. He knew that He would give you faith in your fear, hope in your heart, love in your loss, and peace in your pain.

> God has a purpose and a plan for your life.

DAY FIFTEEN

[27 Peace I leave with you; my peace I give you. I do not give to you as the world gives. Do not let your hearts be troubled and do not be afraid.]

John 14:27

Pregnancy and infant loss can prove to grievers how little control we have on the circumstances in our lives. I'm a bit of a control freak (something I'm working on getting under control) and I sometimes get worried and anxious when things aren't going my way, especially when it's something out of my hands. Traffic was an anxious trigger for me. Living in a big city, notorious for traffic congestion, has taught me a bit about peace. I would leave my full time job in the hot, Los Angeles valley and drive 18 miles across town to classes at my college downtown. I went to school after work Monday through Thursday and this simple 18-mile journey would normally take about an hour. If there was construction, an accident, or a big event on the route, this same 18 mile path could easily double to two hours. Spending over a couple of hours of your life nearly every day of the week inside of a metal box of a car is enough to drive the sanest saint insane. I knew that if I didn't find some peace about the traffic that always awaited me daily, I would have to quit school and give up on my goals because I allowed the anxiety of what I couldn't control get the best of me. I used the time to decompress from my workday by talking to God about what was on my mind, listening to classical music, and calling friends and family who I normally don't [Christ has given peace.] get a chance to talk to. The world gives trouble, unrest, roadblocks, and detours. Christ has given peace. The peace we have gives us the courage to press forward in our grief. Ultimately, we had no control over the outcome of our pregnancy, but we can allow God to guard and restore our hearts with the perfect peace that comes from Him.

PEACE PRACTICE #2

Something that really helped me to release a lot of my emotions following my pregnancy loss was to create an emotional mind map. I immediately felt better once I wrote my feelings down and began to change the way I viewed it so that I could start my healing process.

You can download and print the journal for this book, (www.YourPeaceJourney.com) which has the diagrams illustrated for you. Fold a sheet of paper, draw a circle and write "pregnancy loss" inside the circle as shown. Surround the circle with all of the emotions you personally associated with your loss. Some of mine included: sad, empty, traumatic, broken, anger, why?, ashamed, confused... and so many more. Next, flip the paper, draw a circle, and write "pregnancy gain" inside. On this side of the page, write what you have gained from your experience. This may be difficult for some as it was for me. Originally, my "pregnancy loss" side significantly outweighed my "pregnancy gain" side. It took time but I still revisit my mind map to add to my "pregnancy gain." My gains include: a closer relationship with my husband, more study of God's word, becoming an author (a major life goal of mine), being a survivor, greater appreciation of life, knowing I am not alone...and the list keeps growing.

EMOTIONAL MIND MAP

_____   _____   _____

_____   _____   _____

_____   _____   _____

_____   _____

_____   Pregnancy   _____
            Loss
_____   _____

_____   _____

_____   _____   _____

_____   _____   _____

_____   _____   _____

_____   _____   _____

EMOTIONAL MIND MAP

--- --- ---

--- --- ---

--- --- ---

--- ---

--- ---

--- (Pregnancy Gain) ---

--- ---

--- ---

--- --- ---

--- --- ---

--- --- ---

PRAYER

I need you God. You who have overcome the world, I need that same power in my life. I need you to take the reins of my life and direct me in your way and in your path. I will wait for you as I give up control so that I am not consumed by my loss. Your word tells me that your compassions never fail and I believe it. Daily I awake to new compassion knowing that your love is great and mighty. I trust that you will meet all of my needs because you have glorious riches. Replace my fear with faith. Search my heart and fill the emptiness with your love, joy and peace. Thank you for my hope, my future, my prosperity, your compassion, and the overflow of your blessings.
Amen.

P

E

[A]ct

C

E

DAY SIXTEEN

[
¹⁰ sorrowful, yet always rejoicing; poor,
yet making many rich; having nothing,
and yet possessing everything.
]

II Corinthians 6:10

Following my loss, I was extremely sad. My emotions were so deep that I questioned if I would ever get out of my funk. I even felt guilty if I laughed at something funny on TV or if a friend told a joke to try to cheer me up. I didn't know how to balance my joy and pain. I felt as if it had to be one or the other and my pain was winning. The truth was that, despite my loss, I had numerous reasons to rejoice. Having joy does not diminish the love you feel for your baby.

> Having joy does not diminish the love you feel for your baby.

DAY SEVENTEEN

[^{22} A cheerful heart is good medicine, but a crushed spirit dries up the bones.]

Proverbs 17:22

Not knowing what was before me, I entered my scheduled prenatal appointment with a full belly, and joy from anticipation of the expected arrival of my baby boy. Three days later, I was left empty with a crushed spirit. I felt like I had a storm cloud above my head. At the hospital, they constantly try to keep your comfort level in check by offering painkillers but nothing they had could take away the deep pain within me. Joy is a medicine that can help in our healing. In your experience of just how short and precious life is, you have to give yourself permission to smile. Particularly in times when it seems as if there is absolutely nothing to smile about, you must find a smile somewhere. Anywhere. You can choose to be an active participant in your healing.

> Give yourself permission to smile.

DAY EIGHTEEN

37 No, in all these things we are more than conquerors through him who loved us. 38 For I am convinced that neither death nor life, neither angels nor demons, neither the present nor the future, nor any powers, 39 neither height nor depth, nor anything else in all creation, will be able to separate us from the love of God that is in Christ Jesus our Lord.

Romans 8:37-39

The love that God has for us is limitless. People let us down all the time. I'm sure modern medicine and doctors have disappointed us in our respective situations. In all of our downs, God continuously raises us up. In Him, we are more than conquerors. We are victorious. We are victorious over grief, victorious over depression, victorious over heartache and victorious over pain.

> In Him, we are more than conquerors.

God loves us so much that He gave up His son to die for us so that we could have access to Him. Certainly our God is compassionate towards us in that He also lost a son. Just as Christ conquered death, we are also conquerors. What shall we do with this victory? What shall we do with this love? We love deeply because we are deeply loved. If we didn't love, we wouldn't be so affected by our unfortunate loss. Love is an important part of our healing. Love is an action. God loved us so much that He *gave*. He gave life. You can expand on the great love you have for your baby by showing love to others. Your spouse, parents, brother, sister, niece, and nephew all lost a family member. Just as nothing of this world can separate us from the love of God, we should make sure that we don't allow our loss to separate us from the love we show family and friends in our time of healing.

DAY NINETEEN

[¹⁷ In the same way, faith by itself, if it is
not accompanied by action, is dead.]

James 2:17

When I was pregnant, I was always on the go. I worked full time, went to school part time, took aqua zumba classes (very fun!), pre-natal yoga classes (I felt so very California) and I made sure to have time to hang out with my husband and my friends. When my loss occurred, everything came to a screeching halt. I felt like a walking zombie as I struggled to understand this major detour my life had taken. Instead of co-workers, classes, and conversation, I preferred to sob in my bed with the blinds drawn closed. I fully understood the expression, "shell of oneself" because that is what I had become, a shell, emptied of my former energetic self. This was not how I wanted to live. Even though my outlook was bleak, I had faith that I still had a future. With a future comes purpose and even though I didn't feel like it, I had to take the steps to act on my faith. The steps I took were very small. I began with opening the blinds, going for walks, writing, and slowly introducing myself back to the world. I'm sure my little angel baby would not want his mama drowning in sorrow. Take action in your healing. You don't have to do it alone. Talk with family and friends about your feelings and what you have been through. Make an appointment with a licensed therapist to help you sort through your emotions. Your future will be glad you did.

> Take action in your healing.

DAY TWENTY

> 10 For we are God's handiwork, created
> in Christ Jesus to do good works,
> which God prepared in advance for us
> to do.

Ephesians 2:10

We were created for greatness.
God in His unmatchable power
created you. You were not an acci-

> You were created with intention and with purpose.

dent. You were created with intention and with purpose.
God knows each and every step that you take. You must
decide what actions you are going to take along your path.
Going through such a personal loss can be a great detour
to your faith and purpose. No matter your situation, you
are still here and you are still His creation and His love. As
His creation, your purpose still remains. We don't do good
works to gain God's love, but we do them in response to
God's love. You may have to pull yourself together piece
by piece. You can hand your fragile heart to God so that
you can allow Him to mend it and fill it so that you can
continue walking your path in Christ, overflowing with
the good works that He has for you to do.

PEACE PRACTICE #3

I have a confession to make. I don't really exercise. I love swimming, surfing, and any activity that has to do with water but I definitely don't exercise as often as I would like. In my efforts to maintain a healthy pregnancy, I took prenatal yoga classes and aqua zumba classes but that all stopped after the pregnancy was over. We all know that exercising has great benefits but I'm sure a lot of people have plenty of excuses not to exercise: no time, no money, or even no time and no money.

My challenge to you is to grab a bottle of water and take a walk. Actually go outside (not to your dusty tread-mill), breathe deeply, and walk around the block of your neighborhood. Take notice of the trees, birds, sights, and sounds. Be completely aware and present with your surroundings. This won't cost you anything and it can take 20 minutes. I hope you return home invigorated, refreshed, and uplifted.

PRAYER

God, the feelings that accompanies loss can sometimes be too much to bear. However, I have faith that you are able to heal my heart. In believing that you will mend my heart, I ask that you give me the strength and courage to have joy. Doctors have no magic pill for a broken heart, but your prescription instructs me to have cheer. Please lift my spirit. Lift my head and remind me that I am more than a conqueror in you. Show me and help me to live out your will in my life. Allow me the capacity to embrace and reap the benefits of both grief and joy so that I live my life to the fullest.
Amen.

P
E
A
[C]hange
E

DAY TWENTY-ONE

[
² Do not conform to the pattern of
this world, but be transformed by the
renewing of your mind. Then you will
be able to test and approve what God's
will is—his good, pleasing and perfect
will.
]

Romans 12:2

When going through pregnancy loss, it can be quite normal for your mind to wonder what you could have done differently, or if there was something that you missed that could have saved your baby's life, or even if you did something in the past to deserve such a devastatingly painful loss. Having your mind ramble with such thoughts can keep you in a state of despair and depression. Have you ever seen the *Transformers* movies? In the movie, Transformers are cars that blend in with the rest of the cars driving down the street. Even though these cars look like all others, they are special on the inside, they are set apart. When called upon, they are able to literally transform, to completely change form in order to fight and ultimately win any battle that comes before them. This verse asks you not to blend in, but to transform. How do you transform? You must renew your mind. You must change, and change begins

> You must change, and change begins with what and how you think.

with what and how you think. There is no joy, no peace in pondering over what you have no control over. You can shift your focus to God's plan and purpose for your life.

DAY TWENTY-TWO

[
8 Finally, brothers and sisters, whatever
is true, whatever is noble, whatever
is right, whatever is pure, whatever
is lovely, whatever is admirable—if
anything is excellent or praiseworthy—
think about such things.
]

Philippians 4:8

Can you imagine how positive people would be if we all only thought good thoughts? When I was first hit with the news of my loss, there was not a positive bone in my body. If someone asked me how I was doing, I wouldn't even open my mouth because I knew that they really didn't want to hear what was going on in my head. I would just shrug my shoulders or look off in the distance with tears welling in my eyes as a sign for them to back off before the poor well-intending inquisitor felt the wrath of a very angry and discouraged not-so-mother-to-be. I knew this type of thinking was destructive to my health and well-being and that it was also very isolating. I had to pray that God would heal my pain and hurt and heal my mind so that I wouldn't become a negative, bitter person. Whenever you find yourself thinking thoughts that are negative and unproductive to God's plan for you, you must make a conscious decision to redirect your thoughts to something excellent and worthy of praise. Being positive and

[Be positive and peaceful.]

peaceful in such painful situations will definitely set you apart and show others God's glory in our life.

DAY TWENTY-THREE

> [² Consider it pure joy, my brothers
> and sisters, whenever you face trials
> of many kinds, ³ because you know
> that the testing of your faith produces
> perseverance. ⁴ Let perseverance finish
> its work so that you may be mature
> and complete, not lacking anything.]

James 1:2-4

As long as you are living, you will face many difficult challenges. These challenges will no doubt test your faith in God. Often, you have no control over what happens in life but you *can* control your reaction to your new reality.

[Is your reaction joy?]

Is your reaction joy? Joy was definitely not my first (or fifth, or twentieth) reaction. Joy is usually the last thing on your mind when you are going through difficult times. Is it possible to change your mindset to one that reflects joy instead of despair? When you know that your loss is bigger than you, and that it is an opportunity to develop and mold you into the person that God intended you to be then you can begin to rejoice. You can rejoice because your challenge is an avenue for God to fill your void and shine brightly in your life. You can rejoice because even though you may feel defeated, you know that God is always victorious. You can rejoice because you know that God loves you. You can rejoice because you know that God is hard at work in your life. At times, this may seem unbearable, but He gives you the strength you need to keep holding on.

DAY TWENTY-FOUR

[
³ Not only so, but we also glory in
our sufferings, because we know that
suffering produces perseverance;
⁴ perseverance, character; and
character, hope. ⁵ And hope does not
put us to shame, because God's love
has been poured out into our hearts
through the Holy Spirit, who has been
given to us.
]

Romans 5:3-5

Does this passage sound familiar? This scripture along with James 1:2-4 both encourage you to be joyful in difficult times. This seems like such an oxymoron. This concept of having joy through pain is a foreign concept for most. Perhaps that's the reason why it is reiterated again and again in the Bible. You can begin to look at your loss as a gain. Yes, your loss caused you a lot of hurt and silent suffering. Yes, you experienced sleepless nights with tear-stained pillows. Yes, you felt empty and broken without the hope of life that was once inside. God still asks

[God still asks us to rejoice!]

us to rejoice! How can you rejoice? Your joy comes from the knowledge that your loss was not in vain. Out of your suffering will come strength and the ability to press forward despite your pain. As you persevere, your character is being constructed. Your character is the very essence of your being. It is who you are when no one is looking. Your character is how you think, act, feel, see and react. Do you see the cup as half full or half empty? As a child of the most High, you should see it as running over. You are overflowing with God's love and the hope and expectation that God will fulfill His promises for you.

DAY TWENTY-FIVE

[
16 Therefore we do not lose heart.
Though outwardly we are wasting
away, yet inwardly we are being
renewed day by day. 17 For our
light and momentary troubles are
achieving for us an eternal glory that
far outweighs them all. 18 So we fix
our eyes not on what is seen, but on
what is unseen, since what is seen
is temporary, but what is unseen is
eternal.
]

II Corinthians 4:16-18

It may be hard to look past your pain to the bigger picture of your life. Your trouble is the cause of much change in your life. You can choose to view this change as a good change. Psalm 30:5 says that, "weeping may stay for the night, but rejoicing comes in the morning". This psalm laid heavily on me. I kept waiting for the morning to come because all I did was weep, and night seemed endless. It was not until I focused on trusting that God had nothing but the best intentions for me that I could rejoice in what I couldn't see. You can see that your baby is gone—but what you cannot see is the work that is surrounding this unfortunate event in your life. You cannot see the greatness that God has already produced for your future. Every day you are renewed and restored through Christ. Are you resisting or are you willing to embrace God's restoration?

> Every day you are renewed and restored through Christ.

PEACE PRACTICE #4

Do you ever complain? Do you ever have negative thoughts? We all do, and I'm sure we fill our mind with more negativity than we think. This exercise causes for a total mind shift. Your challenge is to go for a full day with only positive thoughts. It's not as easy as you think. You have to be conscious about every thought that enters your mindspace. Capture and stop any negative thoughts and replace them with positive ones. If it is raining and storming outside, don't say that its bad weather, instead thank God that you don't have to water your lawn. Are you stuck in traffic? Instead of honking and complaining, take the time to listen to an audio book or a podcast. Try this for a full day. Examine how you feel at the end of the day. Try to expand this process for multiple days.

PRAYER

Father, my pain is great, but I know that you are greater. I pray that you transform my mind. Turn my focus from the negative to rejoicing in the positive. Shift my thoughts to things that are excellent and praiseworthy. Show me the joy in my trials. Mold me and shape me in your hands in this time so that I develop into a better person than I was before. Renew my mind, body, and spirit as you direct me through the changes that life brings. Bring me the peace I need to make it through the storms of life.
Amen.

P

E

A

C

[E]ncourage

DAY TWENTY-SIX

[17] The righteous cry out, and the Lord
hears them;
he delivers them from all their
troubles.
[18] The Lord is close to the
brokenhearted
and saves those who are crushed in
spirit.

Psalm 34:17-18

There aren't many words that can describe how a person feels when they lose a child, but I think that "broken-hearted" is an appropriate one. If brokenhearted can mean that "my heart was ripped out of my chest, flash frozen, and hammered into a billion tiny fragile pieces, all screaming in pain and disbelief" then yes, I would say that "broken-hearted" is a great adjective for how I feel. Thankfully we have a God who is close to us. God does not turn His back on you in your distress; He does the opposite, He reaches for you. He delivers you. How amazing is that? There are many different directions you can take in your grief. The devil would love to see you turn to drinking to numb your pain. The adversary wants you to unleash your anger on your loved ones causing discord and rifts in your relationships. God gives us free will in every choice we make. It is my encouragement to you that you choose God. Choose love. Choose faith. Choose peace. Choose hope. Choose with the knowledge that God is there to mend your broken heart. He knows where each piece fell when your heart was shattered. He knows because He created you and He created your emotions and feelings. He saw the trauma you faced. He wants you to know that you are not alone. He is close to you. He will deliver you from your distress.

> Thankfully we have a God who is close to us.

DAY TWENTY-SEVEN

[
¹⁰ Each of you should use whatever gift
you have received to serve others, as
faithful stewards of God's grace in its
various forms.
]

I Peter 4:10

The experiences you have in life prepare you for your purpose. Losing a baby affects each person differently depending on your background, circumstances, support, physical and mental health, as well as a number of other factors. Just as no two pregnancies are alike, no two pregnancy losses are alike. There is no way you can know exactly what the next person is going through with her loss. You can, however, be there for others in their time of need. You can listen without judgment being empathetic and compassionate to those emotions that you know all too well. You have a great responsibility as one who continues to persevere to help others through their grief. You may have lost, but you have also gained so much in your experience. Your new outlook, your new perspective and your new normal can be a blessing and a light to those who need help navigating thought such a dark time.

[Be a blessing and a light to others.]

DAY TWENTY-EIGHT

> [3] Praise be to the God and Father
> of our Lord Jesus Christ, the Father
> of compassion and the God of all
> comfort, [4] who comforts us in all our
> troubles, so that we can comfort those
> in any trouble with the comfort we
> ourselves receive from God.

II Corinthians 1:3-4

I'm sure you learned a great deal about yourself and about God in your loss. You didn't know how strong and how resilient you could be. You went through your own personal grieving

> You didn't know how strong and how resilient you could be.

process for your little one, or you are still going through it. God freely gives comfort to your heart and soul. He acts with the greatest compassion that you need in your life. He moves and shapes your life in such an awesome way that you can't help but to praise Him. Since you have been shown comfort, you are called to comfort others in their trouble times. Because we live, everyone will have some experience with death and loss at some point. The same comfort that is given to you should be extended to those you know, who also need to be comforted. You don't have the power to "fix-it" or to take away their trouble but you can offer a shoulder to cry on. You can remember ways that others helped you in your time of need that were beneficial. From your experience, you know to stay away from saying things that were well-intended but hurtful to you when you were grieving. You can simply supply hugs and prayers knowing that they, like you, can make it through and encourage them to keep fighting the good fight of faith with God's strength.

DAY TWENTY-NINE

[²⁸ And we know that in all things God
works for the good of those who love
him, who have been called according
to his purpose.]

Romans 8:28

I know a lot of people hate math (I actually love it!) but I think that we can all agree that math is something that we can't escape. Let's say that you work a job that pays $20 per hour. Last week, you worked 40 hours at this job. Before your check is even written, and cashed in your head, you can do your own math:

$$\$20 \times 40 \text{ hours} = \$800 \text{ gross income}$$

Now if your check was shorted, you would have to have a little, calm, sit-down discussion with the payroll department. This familiar passage in Romans reads like a math equation to me:

You (you love God; you are called
according to His purpose)
+
Loss (trauma, pain, grief, fear, broken,
hopelessness, emptiness… etc)
=
God ensures that it all works together for good

We may never know "why" we went through such terrible circumstances, but just as we know for sure that $2+2=4$, we know for sure that God works everything out for good. As I write this, I'm seven weeks post partum and as I struggle to wrap my brain around the events that have taken place in my life, I hold on to the promise that God has not given up on me. God has not given up on you. He can take what the devil meant for your destruction and cause it all to come together for good.

DAY THIRTY

[
¹¹ You turned my wailing into dancing;
you removed my sackcloth and
clothed me with joy,
¹² that my heart may sing your praises
and not be silent.
Lord my God, I will praise you
forever.
]

Psalm 30:11-12

In biblical times, people mourned a lot differently than they do today in western culture. One sign that someone was in mourning was that they put on sackcloth. An example is seen in Genesis 37:34 when Jacob was in mourning for his son, Joseph, where Jacob tore his clothes in grief and put on sackcloth. We may not wear sackcloth now, but while we are grieving, we "wear" our sadness, tears, depression, fear, anger, anxiety, brokenness, sorrow, and any other emotion we may be feeling at the time. God is able to walk with you through your mourning and replace it with joy! When He takes you from pain and sorrow to a place of peace and joy, you can't help but to praise His name. Others can be encouraged because they know what you have been through. They know because you can tell others your testimony of where you were to where He has brought you. Be encouraged that the same God that transformed David's wailing to dancing and his sackcloth to joy can, and will do the same for you.

> God is able to walk with you through your mourning and replace it with joy!

DAY THIRTY-ONE

[¹⁵ Rejoice with those who rejoice; mourn with those who mourn.]

Romans 12:15

Grief is one of those interesting things in life, because it is something that everyone experiences, yet no one knows how to deal with it. My father died when I was very young and even though a great deal of time has passed, he is still not forgotten and my grief for him is not something that I ever "got over." Growing up without my father greatly affected my life in more ways than I care to count. Death and loss is hard and sad, no matter what stage of life it may have happened. It is perfectly okay for you to mourn your loss. Mourning can take different forms and different lengths. Grief is not something that you get over, but it is something that you go through. In your healing you can learn to cope and respect the process you are going through. You can also learn how to help, and mourn with others who may find themselves experiencing traumatic loss. You can tap into your own feelings in order to offer a judge-free healing haven as you not only cry for others, but that you cry with them in their dark times.

> Grief is not something that you get over, but it is something that you go through.

PEACE PRACTICE #5

It's not all about you. That was a hard pill for me to swallow that my husband told me once when I was completely comfortable in wallowing in the depths of "Why me?" This world needs you. I know that women are natural nurturers and givers but we sometimes get so caught up in our own world of problems and busyness that we forget about others who aren't in our immediate circle. Do something good for someone. Preferably, choose someone who you aren't super close to. It can be something as simple as picking up the phone and calling (not a text but a real phone call) an old friend or family member whom you haven't spoken to in a while. You can choose a name on your church's sick and shut-in list and mail a card or visit. Volunteer with a charity whose mission you support. There is a great blessing in being a blessing to others.

PRAYER

Lord, I come to you for my broken heart. Cover me with the peace of knowing that you work everything out for my good as I share that peace with those suffering from a broken heart. Remove my sackcloth and clothe me with joy. I need to feel the closeness of your comfort as it prepares me to be of comfort to others in their time of need. Help me to uplift those who are overwhelmed with grief. Give me the wisdom to inhale the goodness of your word and to exhale love, joy, peace, and blessings. Thank you for your matchless compassion. Thank you for your unmerited favor. Thank you for your infinite love. Thank you. Amen.

MY HUSBAND'S STORY

How do I begin to discuss the impact preeclampsia has had on the lives of my wife and me in such a short period of time? Not only did our son pass away, but my wife's life was threatened by the extremely high blood pressure she suddenly developed without any noticeable signs or warnings. Other than it being our first pregnancy, my wife didn't have any of the indicators or risk factors for preeclampsia. Previous check-ups indicated that the pregnancy was progressing normally and our son was healthy and active. I couldn't comprehend the full weight of the situation as things unfolded before us in the blink of an eye. My thoughts were focused on trying to calm and comfort my wife while hoping the doctors had just made a mistake. What do you mean you can't find his heartbeat? The doctors' faces clearly expressed what they were saying and thinking.

Our son's delivery had to occur quickly to reduce the threat to my wife's life. It was very strange experiencing, what I would expect to be, the typical excitement of the labor and delivery process while also knowing that the child being born isn't alive. I proudly encouraged my wife through the delivery process and cut our son's chord. I held our son for the first and last time to say hello and goodbye to him all at the same time. I can still feel the weight of his head in my left hand as I prayed while holding him.

My mind and emotions became the rope in the tug-of-war between the natural feelings of joy and excitement of delivery and the immediate grief that we were now experiencing.

The passing of our son has been a very humbling and mind expanding experience. Not very long ago my dreams were about him growing through the various stages of life. In fact, my wife told me that one night while I was asleep, I expressed out loud that it was great being a father. During the drive home from work, I would frequently think about the days when I'd hear his little feet running to the door when I made it home. I really looked forward to being a father and the adventures that surely were to come.

This experience truly has shown me how small and weak I really am. There was nothing that I could do in it all to change anything. I was along for the ride and needed something secure to hold onto.

The love, support, and encouragement, of friends and family is very important and comforting during the healing process. I also found myself reading and reflecting on the trials that the families of Job and Abraham faced. In those challenges, faithfulness and patience were rewarded greatly with peace and joy.

I've accumulated a number of scars during my short life. Sometimes I think of the scars as God blessing me with an adventurous life. We find ourselves confronted with painful situations that bruise, batter, and otherwise injure us, sometimes deeply and seriously. The pain remains for a while even though we attend to the wounds and begin the healing process. There is a point during the healing where the pain will ease and often fade into our memories. Some wounds heal as scars that serve as a reminder of what we've come through. Sometimes the scars stir up painful memories and sometimes they strengthen us as reminders of victory. I'm sure that this experience will leave a scar in the lives of my wife and me; however, I hope that we'll be able to look back at them as reminders of victory and the goodness of God.

CONCLUSION

Prayer is essential in your walk of faith. For relationships to be successful, you have to communicate effectively. Prayer is your communication with God. When you pray, you can go to God with your thanks, your requests, and on the behalf of others. We serve a big God who is able to answer our big prayers--Prayers for healing, for strength, for direction, for joy, for peace. He is waiting for you to bring it all to Him.

It's not easy, but it is beneficial if you learn to trust God and give Him your fears so that you can walk by faith. God is close to the brokenhearted but we have to be close to Him for it all to work out for good. We don't give a second thought in trusting with our life that a traffic light is working properly as we approach a busy intersection but we are hesitant to trust God with our worries, anger, bitterness, and with our hearts. God can handle ALL of you because He created you.

I'm sure you are familiar with the phrase, "fake it until you make it." I've mentioned how after my loss, I felt very ashamed. I was ashamed and I felt like a failure. The few times I did leave the house, I would walk with my head so low, looking at the ground. It felt like every time I looked up, I would see an abundance of glowing, big belly ladies and new moms taunting me with their fancy three-wheeled strollers carrying chubby-cheeked babies. Often people would see my still swollen stomach and ask when I was due. These feelings and encounters quickly turned me into a hermit. Anyone who knows me knows that I enjoy being out and about. Staying inside and stuck in a destructive mindset is not a very healthy way to live. It is certainly not the way a King's daughter should live. I decided that I would have to fake it until I made it. I didn't feel like facing the world but it took gradual steps for me to re-introduce myself and to walk with my head held high knowing that I had nothing to be ashamed of. My experience is simply another chapter of my life. Everyone goes through obstacles and trials in life. The difference between you and them is the God you serve. You are a royal priesthood. You can decide to walk and act like you are a member of a royal family.

Transformation is key in your healing process. Pregnancy loss changes you. You may change a little or a lot, or better or worst but you will change. How you change is all up to you. Change begins in your heart and in your mind. Transforming your mind doesn't happen overnight, but with time, prayer, and connection to God, you can gain a peace that goes far beyond the usual limits of human understanding.

As you experience God's transformation in your life by bringing you to peace, you can share your joy with others. You can encourage others to walk with Him through their struggles, grief, trials and tribulations. Your truth can be a testimony in helping others along their course.

It is my prayer that this book helped you to tap into your emotions and recognize the vast promises of God. I hope that the verses used will bless you as much as they have blessed me. This book is just one tool that will be used in your journey to peace. I urge you to talk with your friends, family, and even to a licensed counselor about what you have been through. Take notes and write your own story in the complementary journal download that accompanies this book (www.YourPeaceJourney.com). Your journey may not always be easy, but with the Prince of Peace as the ruler of your life, your possibility of peace is endless.

A NOTE FROM THE AUTHOR

I encourage you to consider talking with a licensed therapist or counselor. Join a support group catered to people who have experienced pregnancy loss. Sip some tea. Breathe. Love yourself. Love others.

This book is not intended to be a substitute for the medical advice of your health care provider. Please consult your with your doctor about your specific situation and medical or psychological conditions and needs.

If you feel you are in a crisis and that you may do harm to yourself, contact:

Suicide Prevention Lifeline

1-800-273-TALK (8255)

LET'S CONNECT

Thank you for pursing peace with me. Please take a brief moment to write a review online about your experience with this book. If you like my book, please recommend it to your family and friends.

YourPeaceJourney.com
GoldPeachPress.com

ABOUT THE AUTHOR

Keanna Barnes was completely blindsided with the still-birth of her son. After bouts of depression and despair, she gained the strength to share her story in an effort to show others that they are not alone in their struggles to cope with such tragic circumstances. Her mission is to point the brokenhearted to Christ, the source of unlimited love and peace. Keanna is from Atlanta and currently lives in Los Angeles with her husband where, by the grace of God, they are still healing--together.

CPSIA information can be obtained
at www.ICGtesting.com
Printed in the USA
LVOW13s1744090317
526681LV00010BA/550/P

9 780997 905700